Happy Birthday, al —

Bob Stone
Feb 2, 1971

THE LAST CAPRICE

A book of wills,
odd and curious,
of the famous
and infamous

BY ROBERT S. MENCHIN

With a Foreword by
MORRIS L. ERNST

SIMON AND SCHUSTER, NEW YORK, 1963

SECOND PRINTING
Library of Congress Catalog Card Number: 63-13767
Manufactured in the United States of America
Printed by The Murray Printing Company, Forge Village, Mass.
Bound by Book Press, Inc., Brattleboro, Vermont

FOR
MARYLIN
JONATHAN
AND
SCOTT

Contents

THE LAST CAPRICE

Foreword

The sad and humorous episodes which make up this volume defy an ordinary approach to will-making. Simplification in wills is quite impossible, because no one, no matter what he may think, is a simple person. Life is complicated. That is one of its pleasures. Those who look for simple formulas or wider generalization end up in trouble, for each testator is a separate and unique gathering of cells.

The Last Caprice of each and every human being represents a monopoly, since most of us express ridicule for all caprices except our own. But this book may be a "How to Do It" insofar as it may evoke admiration for the kind of bravery that allows the suppressions of a lifetime to be defiantly proclaimed in a will. After all, says the testator, who can hurt me in the grave?

Jurisprudence may be able to standardize warehouse receipts or check forms, but wills continue to reflect the diversity of man's personality. As a lover of variety and individuality, I suggest we are fortunate to have in this book of fascinating and entertaining stories: the man who took God in as a business partner; the many people who defy death in their own special way by writing their will in verse or treating their will as a practical joke; not to mention the young man who literally swallowed an objectionable will. My own personal favorite is the man who would disown his natural son if he grew a mustache.

Caprice? Perhaps. But where there are few Last Caprices you can be sure the culture is less than free, the income is meager, ambition for better standards of living has not yet been born, and the people are without aspirations, frustrations or ulcers. In many societies today—in parts of Africa and India, for example—possessions can be put into a small ditty bag, and the complicated problems of disposing of one's worldly goods do not arise. Wills are for the sophisticates of our planet.

For nearly half a century as a member of the bar, I have advised a good number of these "sophisticates" and helped them draw wills. We usually begin by reviewing their lists of beneficiaries, and I marvel at the wild conglomeration of conflicting desires and the compromises between love and hate that such a list represents.

In a lawyer's office, Will Time is an occasion for unmasking and for all kinds of spiritual undressing. As each client concedes his mortality and faces up to the problems of disposition, the lawyer's desk becomes the psychologist's couch. Face to face, many of the wealthy who have hated the government give instructions which make bequests to the state and Federal treasuries—in the form of inheritance taxes—rather than leave the money to a pet charity or cause. Then there is the dominant male, often a delightful and casual philanderer, who expresses a desire to have his dead hand control the love life of his surviving wife. She is to receive substantial income until the day of her remarriage. Thus does the testator induce his widow to live in so-called "sin" with a lush income from the estate rather than get married to an impecunious male and have her income cut off.

However, in our society wives may not be totally disowned; even husbands often may not be cut off without a sou. This so-called "dower" is the sovereign state's answer to the testator, preventing the too great expression of hate that would leave the surviving spouse without that guessed-at compromise between duty and affection—often, one-third of the will-maker's estate.

At Will Time, parents are confronted with the fact that all offspring are not equally loved. Then begins the attempt to balance the books—emotional as well as financial.

In this collection of odd and curious wills, the foolish and the wise share a common defiance of the inevitable. While their presence in this book strongly suggests that they are no longer with us, it is a lively and colorful cast of characters that Bob Menchin offers. It is ironic that many relatively unknown and unsung testators may, through this book, be more frequently quoted in death than they ever were in life.

—MORRIS L. ERNST

Nantucket, Mass.
June 1962.

"...must say, before I begin, that the deceased had a most delicious sense of humor."

Introduction

In 1720, an Englishman named Edmund Curll published a curious and now very rare book containing the wills of celebrated personalities of his time. Writing a few hundred years before the heyday of the gossip columnist, Curll was a worthy forerunner of the genre. He would spice his books with biographical sketches, lively anecdotes and intimate facts in the lives of the will-makers—all designed to fan the imagination of the public and provide the subject of conversation at every pub in England. A prominent statesman of his day described Curll as "one of the new terrors of death."

Obviously, he was not without readers.

Wills continue to have a special appeal to those who find the contemplation of human nature a worthy pastime. Perhaps more than any other human document they reflect the character of the writer and reveal his relationship with family, friends and the world at large. His nature, his prejudice, his interests, his eccentricities and the full range of man's virtues and vices can be found in the pages of wills.

When that man happens to be one of history's immortals, the interest is heightened. When, for example, William Shakespeare says in his will that he leaves his wife his "second best bed," he is inviting the raised eyebrow and whispered innuendo for ages to come.

When Benjamin Franklin bequeathed to his son William certain land holdings in Nova Scotia, explaining, "The part he acted against me in the late war, which is of public notoriety, will account for my leaving him no more of an estate he endeavored to deprive me of," we sense the deep chasm that developed between father and son.

And is there anything written by or said about Rabelais, the fifteenth-century satirist, that is as quickly revealing as his one-sentence last will and testament? "I have nothing, I owe a great deal; the rest I give to the poor."

If these choice morsels from the past lead you to conclude that will-writing is a dying art, you have made a weak pun but a fairly perceptive observation. Wills just aren't what they used to be. Virtually all wills today are formal legal documents that only a relative or close friend could find interesting. Resigned to the fact that they cannot take it with them, will-makers approach the problem of giving it away with precision, solemnity and understandable ill-humor. This conventional approach to will-writing simplified matters for the lawyers, the surrogates and the heirs but for the rest of us, it takes all the fun out of minding other people's business. The sameness of format and contents—give or take a few thousand or a few million—makes most wills hopelessly dull. The fact that they enrich someone other than ourselves makes them downright annoying.

Happily, there are those cherished few who break from convention and strike a highly individualistic note. When that happens, as in the case of John B. Kelly, the results can be something special—a collector's delight. The Kelly document stands as eloquent proof that a will need not be prosaic, that a will can be warm, personal and witty without defeating its purpose or endangering its legal status.

Perhaps others, inspired by this classic will and encouraged by the great interest it has evoked, will take advantage of the similar opportunity available to them. But do not take Kelly's "I will attempt to write my own will" literally or be misled by the informal language and casual tone. Kelly drew his will with the cooperation and advice of his attorney—as should you.

That's as far as we go on this point. Other books, and there are many, explain why it is important that you have a will, discuss the legal considerations as they differ in each of the fifty states and issue proper warning against preparing a will without the benefit of legal advice. *The Last Caprice* has a more frivolous purpose.

While I cherish each of the bits and pieces that went into the mosaic that follows, a void remains. The missing wills, the unknown and unheralded fragments that leave the picture incomplete, lie somewhere, gathering dust and slowly disintegrating, surrounded by millions of other wills, embedded in billions of words, and the task of sifting the worthy ones from the unworthy is somewhat akin to isolating a few grams of gold from thousands of tons of rock.

Unlikely Heirs

That so few now dare to be eccentric marks the chief danger of our time.

JOHN STUART MILL

Conrad Cantzen was a familiar figure along Broadway. A gentleman-pauper and actor of bit parts, he panhandled for meals, discreetly snatched food where he could, wore fingerless gloves and a filched boutonniere. When he died in 1945 at the age of seventy-eight, the Actor's Fund paid his hospital bill and buried him in its plot in Kensico Cemetery.

A will was discovered in his dismal, solitary room a few days after he was buried. It began:

I leave the Conrad Cantzen Shoe Fund for the people who can't buy shoes, even if they are not paid-up members of

Equity. Many times I have been on my uppers, and the thinner the soles of my shoes were, the less courage I had to face the managers in looking for a job.

Along with the will went the sum of $226,608.34, a hundred thousand dollars of it in savings banks, the rest in government and gilt-edge bonds. Altogether almost a quarter of a million dollars.

Today any professional actor, temporarily at liberty and making the rounds in a pair of run-down shoes, can "do the shoe bit"—a commonplace experience in Broadway circles. Doing the shoe bit starts with a visit to Actors Equity, at 226 West Forty-seventh Street, and culminates with a visit to the Thom McAn Shoe Store at 129 West Forty-second Street. Compliments of Conrad Cantzen, Actor.

Jack Luke of Rotheringham, England, who died in 1812, left a penny to every child who attended his funeral (over seven hundred youngsters were there). All the poor women in the parish were left one shilling each and the bell ringers were left half a guinea each, to "strike off one peal of grand bobs" at the exact moment of his burial.

Mr. Luke's final bequest was for forty dozen penny loaves which were to be thrown down from a parish church steeple at noon on every Christmas Day forever.

Bread bequests were once popular as Christmas legacies in England. In the year 1660 a pastor named Arthur

Colfe left in trust money to buy 104 sweet penny loaves for the neediest in East London's slum district of Deptfford. Three hundred years of interest has swelled the fund to the point where today, instead of a penny loaf, the beneficiary is entitled to a two-shilling (twenty-eight-cent) voucher for the purchase of food.

One charity bequest calls for the baking of a huge plum pudding, to weigh in excess of three hundred pounds, for needy families in the Devonshire town of Paignton. This bequest, however, comes only once in fifty years. The last plum pudding was distributed in 1951; the next is due in 2001.

In the nineteenth century a man named McAllister, residing in southern Scotland, left each of his daughters her weight in one-pound bank notes. By this provision, one daughter, being considerably stouter than the other, received the equivalent of thirty thousand dollars more than her sister.

Under a century-old legacy provided for by a man named John Orr, interest on an approximately four-thousand-dollar fund is set aside annually for four Scotch brides. Checks to the equivalent of thirty dollars each are sent to the tallest, shortest, oldest and youngest bride married during the year at St. Cyprus, Scotland.

William Berns, a wealthy Madison Avenue jeweler, died on April 20, 1962. According to the terms of his will, his estate, valued at $250,000, goes to the United States Treasury "for general governmental purposes." The will reads:

I make this bequest in appreciation of the freedom and liberty afforded in this country to all citizens, irrespective of race, creed or color.

Berns wrote these words on January 24, 1961, four days after President Kennedy, in his inauguration address, said to the American people, "Ask not what your country can do for you—ask what you can do for your country."

In a will made in 1434, a member of the Norton family of Southwick, London, left all he had "to be used unto the end of the world for the benefit of the poor, the hungry, the thirsty, the naked, the sick, and the wounded, and prisoners," and he appointed the Houses of Parliament as his executors.

The will was set aside on the ground that the testator was insane and the estate was transferred to the natural heirs.

On December 6 and 7, 1922, a total of 203 persons entered the Oakland court of Judge E. S. Robinson to claim their share of a $350,000 bequest left by San Francisco nightclub-owner Joseph Bisagno. Among the heirs were society women, waitresses, matrons, bootblacks, headwaiters, actresses (Broadway star Marjorie Rambeau), waiters, hat-check girls, judges, attorneys, physicians, businessmen, city officials, cafe owners, bartenders and saloonkeepers. All, said Mr. Bisagno in his will, "friends who have been kind to me."

"Jameson, you scoundrel, you've been editing my will again!"
Courtesy Burr Shafer

Unable to make up his mind about which of his three deserving nephews to make his heir, Henry Durrell decided to let fate decide the matter. In his will he stipulated that the choice should be made by a throw of the dice.

On March 15, 1921, three young men met at their late uncle's estate in Bermuda to carry out the terms of the will. A pair of dice was passed around and minutes later Richard Durrell emerged as the new owner of the palatial estate on the shore of Hamilton Harbor, the show place of Bermuda.

*

A rich American who died as the last century drew to a close left every dollar he possessed to a chorus girl he used to watch in the theater. He did not know her and the reason he gave in his will for making the bequest was that her turned-up nose amused him.

If you consider this a capricious reason for making a bequest, you may find these two gentlemen, and their reasons for withholding a bequest, more soundly motivated:

Lord Redesale, a lifetime foe of Communism, died in 1958 during his eightieth year of life. He left an estate of $361,000 to be shared by all but one of his daughters. The exception was Jessica, who had named her child Lenin.

Adolph J. Heimbeck, who died on July 10, 1958, wrote in his will:

I leave nothing to my two sisters Hazel and Katherine as they revere Franklin D. Roosevelt and the taxes caused by him more than equalled their share.

When prominent Canadian attorney Charles Millar died, friends asked his former law partner whether Millar left a will.

"I've found some writing in the form of a will," he replied, "but it's not a will—it's a joke. We're searching for the actual will now."

The "joke" turned out to be The Last Will and Testament of Charles Vance Millar and a few months later his former law partner was defending this "joke" in court—and defending it successfully for twelve years against repeated attacks from outraged citizens, disappointed relatives and righteous reformers who "didn't get the joke."

In the will, Millar explains it this way:

This will is necessarily uncommon and capricious because I have no dependents or near relations and no duty rests upon me to leave any property at my death and what I do leave is proof of my folly in gathering and retaining more than I required in my lifetime.

This preamble to Charles Millar's will suggests what follows: twelve clauses consisting mostly of good-natured pranks and a final caper that sent hundreds of

Canadian women off on a raucous race with the stork that is now known as the celebrated "Baby Derby."

Among Millar's pranks:

To the Hon. W. E. Raney, A. M. Orpen and Reverend Samuel D. Chown, each one share in the Ontario Jockey Club providing three years from my death each of them becomes enrolled as shareholders in the share register of the Club. . . .

Dr. Chown and Judge Raney were dedicated foes of all forms of gambling, especially horse racing. Mr. Orpen operated a track in direct competition to the Jockey Club. On August 27, 1927, Dr. Chown and Judge Raney became members of the club, but five minutes later they sold their shares for fifteen hundred dollars each; Mr. Orpen retained his membership.

To each Protestant Minister exercising his clerical functions . . . and to each Orange Lodge in Toronto I give one share of the O'Keefe Brewery Company of Toronto, Limited.

Of the 260 eligible clergymen, 91 accepted their shares. Of the 114 Orange Lodges, 103 did likewise. Most of the beneficiaries under this clause sold their shares and turned the $58.20 they received for each share over to charity.

Clause number nine in the will turned over Millar's home in Jamaica to three acquaintances. These men each had an abiding dislike for one another, so naturally Millar thought it would be a good idea if they lived together for a while.

All this was by way of a curtain-raiser to the fertility farce inspired by the last bequest in Millar's will:

All the rest and residue of my property . . . at the expiration of ten years from my death . . . to the Mother who has . . . given birth in Toronto to the greatest number of children.

Canada was unprepared for the hijinks that followed. Throughout his seventy-three years of life Charles Millar was a prim, painfully proper bachelor, hardly the type who would inspire Canadian ladies to fill the maternity wards to overflowing. But there it was: the courts upheld the bequest, the money was good and the race was on.

Toronto newspapers quickly dubbed the contest "The Stork Derby" and publicized the event with feature stories as the participants carved new notches on their cribs and new entries became all too apparent. As the mothers approached the finish line, box scores were published and Canadians with sporting blood placed wagers and cheered their favorites to greater heights of achievement.

Meanwhile, Millar's second cousins and even more remote relatives hired lawyers to litigate the will out of existence. Contesters of the will claimed that the clause "encouraged immorality" and was "against public policy" but Millar was as good an attorney as he was a prankster. The will was legally sound—again and again the court found in favor of "the unknown mother."

On May 30, 1938, Judge MacDonnell of Surrogate Court, Toronto, distributed the estate. With interest added it came to $568,106. Four prolific Toronto mothers, each with nine children born during the ten-year period, shared the prize in accordance with the terms of the will.

Mrs. Pauline Mae Clark claimed ten births during the period but her record was somewhat marred by the fact that only five children were also her husband's. To settle this sticky situation as well as the claim of Mrs. Lilie Kenny (four of her ten children were stillborn) consolation prizes of $12,500 were awarded to the runners-up.

In the summer of 1936, when she had her last baby, one of the winners, Mrs. Arthur Timleck, announced wearily that she was through: from here on she intended to practice—and preach—birth control. Charlie Millar would have gotten a chuckle out of that.

Everybody knew that Juan Potomachi was stagestruck. But no one realized just how stagestruck Señor Potomachi was until his death in 1955. In his will the Buenos Aires businessman left a part of his fortune to Teatro Dramatico—but on one condition. As he explains in his will:

All my life I wanted to be on the stage. Lack of talent prevented me at first from realizing that wish. Later my position in the community as a prominent businessman barred me altogether from the stage.

30

I leave 200,000 pesos ($50,000) to a fund from which talented young actors shall get yearly scholarships. My only condition is that my head be preserved and used as a skull in Hamlet.

My dearest wish would be thereby fulfilled after all, as I would still have a part in a play after my death.

Odd as this conditional bequest is, it is not unique. John Reed, a gas lighter of the Walnut Street Theater of Philadelphia in the nineteenth century, never, as far as anyone knows, aspired to appear on the stage during his lifetime. He remained on the job for forty-four years, never absent, never late, never missing a performance. His death brought to light an ambition which, unless it was purely coincidental, inspired Señor Potomachi's bequest. A clause in John Reed's will reads as follows:

. . . my head to be separated from my body immediately after my death; the latter to be buried in a grave; the former, duly macerated and prepared, to be brought to the theater where I have served all my life, and to be employed to represent the skull of Yorick in the play Hamlet.

Discouraged by years of failure and defeat, Paul Duhalde, dealer in precious stones, opened his account book to a fresh page, entered the date—September 27, 1719—and wrote these words:

I have resolved to enter into a partnership with God, promising and undertaking to fulfill all the within-mentioned articles; and I enjoin my heirs, whoever they may be, to carry out these my intentions in case I should die before accomplishing them myself.

Shortly thereafter the tide of events changed. Duhalde married the daughter of a wealthy merchant and his business prospered as he gained new skill and confidence as a trader. Never failing to meet his obligations to his silent, invisible partner, Duhalde drew half the profits at regular intervals and distributed them to the poor "in the name of God."

Some ten years after the partnership began, the diamond merchant was struck down with a serious illness. In a hastily prepared will, written in the third person, he said:

In the books which contain the minutes of his affairs there are several articles touching matters that concern the poor; he begs his executor to examine these articles with the greatest accuracy, and to see that they are carried out with the strictest attention.

When Duhalde died two months after making his will, his executors found many packets of precious gems marked "Half for the poor" at the merchant's shop. In his final days Duhalde had expressed the desire that his partner's share, the half for the poor, be given to the Hôpital Général and so the administrators of that institution claimed the bequest.

Duhalde's young widow balked at the idea of sharing the legacy and the dispute had to be resolved in court.

Speaking for the widow, the guardian asked that the will be set aside on the ground that the testator was not mentally competent to draw a will since "no sane man ever entered into partnership with God."

On April 3, 1726, Avocat-Général D'Agnesseau handed down the decision that "the will shall be fulfilled according to the desire of the testator," and directed the widow to hand over to the hospital administrators the jewels constituting the legacy made by the testator—thereby closing the dramatic story of Paul Duhalde, dealer in diamonds, and his singular partnership with God.

The Prince of Darkness had his day in court. A wealthy Finnish landowner left a will bequeathing all of his vast property to the Devil. The will was set aside by the court, the Devil's claim disregarded and the property passed on to the legal heirs.

An old French proverb has it, "The Devil comes to us on wings but goes away limping."

So many wills are made each year with a dumb animal as the principal beneficiary that it can no longer be considered an eccentricity. Nowadays when a will naming a horse, dog, cat, monkey or parrot is admitted to probate, it does not even merit a three-line notice on page 56 of the *Times*.

However, no book on odd wills would be complete without at least one such entry. For the single, singular example, consider the will of Mr. Jonathan Jackson of Columbus, Ohio, who died early in the present century. Mr. Jackson left his money for the erection and maintenance of an elaborate home for cats, and in his will he gives careful, detailed specifications. The building is to contain dormitories, a refectory, areas for conversation, grounds for exercise, gently sloping roofs for climbing, an auditorium where the cat inmates may listen to accordian music, and "rat holes" for daily sport.

The testator gives as the reason for his bequest: "It is man's duty as lord of animals to watch over and protect the lesser and feebler, even as God watches over and protects man."

Why rats, supplied for the "sport" of his cherished cats, should not be entitled to similar protection, Mr. Jackson does not say.

∗

Mr. Daniel Martinett, of Calcutta in the East Indies, was a simple man, a man who "lived profusely and died frugally":

First. In the most submissive manner I recommend my soul to Almighty God, &c.

Secondly. Now as to my worldly concerns, in the following manner: As to this fulsome carcase having already seen enough of worldly pomp, I desire nothing relative to it to be done, only its being stowed away in my old green chest, to avoid expense; for as I lived profusely, I die frugally.

Thirdly. The undertaker's fees come to nothing, as I won them from him at a game of billiards, in the presence of Mr. Thomas Morrice and William Perkes, at the said William Perkes' home, in February last.

Fourthly. To Henry Vansittart, Esq., Governor of Bengal, as an opulent man, I leave the discharge of all such sums of money that I shall stand indebted to indigent persons in the town of Calcutta.

Fifthly. To Mr. George Grey, Secretary to the Presidency, I bequeath all my sincerity.

Sixthly. To Mr. Simon Drose, Writer to the Secretary's office, all my modesty.

Seventhly. To Mr. Henry Higgenson, also of the Secretary's office, all the thoughts I hope I shall die possessed of.

Eighthly. To Mr. Thomas Forbes, all the worldly assurance which I had when I had taken a cheerful glass, though in fact a doleful cup.

As I have lived the make-game of a modern gentleman, being a butt for envy and a mark for malice, by acting a little out of the common road, though, thank God, never in a base way, I hope I may die in sincere love and charity to all men, forgiving all my persecutors, as I hope for forgiveness from my Creator.

As it lies not in my power to bequeath anything to my relations at home, I shall say nothing concerning them, as they have not for these six years past concerned themselves about me; excepting that I heartily wish them all well, and that my brothers and sisters may make a more prosperous voyage through this life than I have done.

(Signed) DANIEL MARTINETT

The original of this will was deposited in the Registry Office at Calcutta after the death of Daniel Martinett in

1825. The Governor accepted the legacy of debts referred to in item four—and paid them!

"And to my brother George Clark, who was always telling me that 'health is more important than wealth,' I leave my rowing machine."

Courtesy Hank Ketcham

A New York tailor who died in 1880 left these instructions in his will:

I own seventy-one pairs of trousers, and I strictly enjoin my executors to hold a public sale, at which these shall be sold to the highest bidder, and the proceeds distributed to the poor of the city.

I desire that these garments shall in no way be examined or meddled with, but be disposed of as they are found at the time of my death; and no purchaser to buy more than one pair.

The sale was actually held and the seventy-one pair of trousers were sold to seventy-one different purchasers. As each purchaser cut the thread to open the pockets, he found a packet containing a thousand dollars in bank notes—a reward, no doubt, for his good taste.

The president of the Colorado Woman's Christian Temperance Union received a bequest of five shares of brewery company stock "as a marker for her family Bible." The stock was willed to the temperance leader in 1934 by Charles F. Hoechel, a Denver printer who was jailed at her insistence for printing liquor lists in violation of a Colorado liquor law.

To a Colorado banker, Mr. Hoechel left six hundred worthless shares in an oil company "which he sold to me on the damnedest misrepresentation and which he can use as a marker for *his* prayer book."

In a will published shortly after his death in 1950, George Bernard Shaw disposed of £367,233 ($1,028,-252), a figure that makes the socialist author a capitalist of magnitude. *My Fair Lady*, the musical version of his play *Pygmalion*, had a seven-year run on Broadway and has been performed in Sweden, Mexico, Germany and Australia. The Shaw estate earned in excess of two million dollars on the Broadway production alone and the sale to the movies for an unprecedented five and a half million dollars will swell the estate beyond the realm of even Shaw's soaring imagination.

The author's detailed fourteen-page will begins with instructions for the cremation of the body. "Personally," he writes in his will, "I prefer the garden to the cloister."

For many years before his death Shaw had been toying with the idea of leaving his estate for the purpose of creating and promoting a new phonetic alphabet which would simplify the spelling of English words and correct the disparity between the spoken word and the written word. Many of his friends felt that this was Shaw's way of dramatizing a cause he felt strongly about and that he would not really leave his money for so frivolous and futile a project. But Shaw meant what he said. Following a number of small personal bequests, the will directed that the residue of the estate should be used to determine how much time and effort could be saved by substituting a new forty-letter phonetic alphabet for the present English alphabet.

The British Museum and the Royal Academy of Dramatic Arts, confined in the use of the money by the specific directions, contested the will on the grounds that the alphabet trust was vague. In 1957, a compromise settlement was reached: only a limited portion of the estate would be used for the alphabet reform plan.

In a competition held shortly after to find a design for the new alphabet, 467 entries were received but not one was considered so outstanding as to merit its adoption as the Proposed British Alphabet. Four entries were chosen worthy of sharing the five-hundred-pound prize and the winners were asked to collaborate with scholars in the field in the hope that a final alphabet would evolve.

If, as, and when the alphabet is created, the real problem will be in gaining acceptance of the new phonetic alphabet by the English-speaking people of the world— a possibility that seems as remote as ever.

The Irish-born wife of playwright George Bernard Shaw left an estate of $263,200. In a long and verbose will (one sentence contained 151 words), Mrs. Shaw expressed the desire that her money be spent teaching her distinguished husband's compatriots "self-control, elocution, deportment, the arts of personal contact and social intercourse."

An eighteenth-century English gentleman apparently considered the Irish beyond reform. His will, probated in 1791, bequeaths the annual sum of ten pounds to be paid out by his estate for the following purpose:

It is my will and pleasure that this sum shall be spent in the purchase of a certain quantity of the liquor vulgarly called whiskey, and it shall be publicly given out that a certain number of persons, Irish only, not to exceed twenty, who may choose to assemble in the cemetery in which I shall be interred, on the anniversary of my death, shall have the same distributed to them. Further, it is my desire that each shall receive it by half-a-pint at a time till the whole is consumed, each being likewise provided with a stout oaken stick and a knife, and that they shall drink it all on the spot.

Knowing what I know of the Irish character, my conviction is, that with these materials given they will not fail to destroy each other, and when in the course of time the race comes to be exterminated, this neighborhood at least may, perhaps, be colonized by civilized and respected Englishmen.

Ella Wendel, a picturesque New York recluse, died in 1931, leaving the bulk of a forty-million-dollar estate to charity. Altogether 2,303 separate claims—mostly by remote relatives—were filed against the will. So many challengers and their attorneys appeared to contest the will that they could not fit into the courtroom at one time.

Among the challengers was Thomas Patrick Morris, who mounted the witness stand and announced that he was the son of Miss Wendel's late brother, and therefore he had prior claim on the estate. Mr. Morris told a dramatic and minutely detailed story of his mother's secret marriage to the dead millionaire and offered in evidence a marriage certificate and a will which made him the sole heir to the Wendel fortune. For weeks the case was featured in front-page headlines and the legacy seemed to be within the reach of Mr. Morris, who confidently told reporters at a press conference that the money would be used "to help people who are poor and passed over by the world."

A small flaw stood between Mr. Morris and his philanthropic aspirations: the Bible in which the marriage certificate was inscribed was printed twenty-four years *after* the date on the certificate.

With that revelation, the case collapsed. The will turned out to be a clever forgery, and the forger a teller of tall tales. Of the 2,303 claimants to the Wendel estate, the court recognized the rights of nine fifth-degree relatives. Among the losers was Thomas Patrick Morris, who was sentenced to three years in the state penitentiary for forging a will worth forty million dollars.

"Now read me the part again where I disinherit everybody."

Drawing by Peter Arno;
© 1940 The New Yorker Magazine, Inc.

Vindictive Wills

Thieves, as a last donation, leave advice to their friends, physicians a nostrum, authors a manuscript work, rakes a confession of their faith in the virtue of the sex—all, the last drivellings of their egotism and impertinence. One might suppose that if anything could, the approach and contemplation of death might bring men to a sense of reason and self-knowledge. On the contrary, it seems only to deprive them of the little wit they had, and to make them even more the sport of their wilfulness and short-sightedness.

WILLIAM HAZLITT, "On Will-making"

From the Last Will and Testament of John Aylett, proved in June 1781, pictorial retribution:

I hereby direct my executors to lay out five guineas in purchase of a picture of the viper biting the benevolent hand of the person who saved him from perishing in the snow, if the same can be bought for the money; and that they do, in memory of me, present it to Edward Bearcroft, Esq., a King's Counsel, whereby he may have frequent opportunities for contemplating on it.

This I direct to be presented to him in lieu of a legacy of three thousand pounds which I had, by a former will, now revoked and burnt, left him.

43

Excerpts from the Last Will and Testament of Philip, Fifth Earl of Pembroke (seventeenth century):

Item: I give my body, for it is plain I cannot keep it; as you see, the chirurgeons are tearing it in pieces. Bury me, therefore; I hold lands and churches enough for that.

Item: I will have no monument, for then I must needs have an epitaph, and verses over my carcase: during my life I have had enough of these.

Item: I give all my wild beasts to the Earl of Salisbury, being very sure that he will preserve them, seeing that he refused the King a doe out of his park.

Item: I give *nothing* to my Lord Saye, and I do make him this legacy willingly, because I know that he will faithfully distribute it unto the poor.

Item: I bequeath to Thomas May, whose nose I did break at a mascarade, five shillings. My intention had been to give him more; but all who shall have seen his *History of Parliament* will consider that even this sum is too large.

Item: I give to the Lieutenant-General Cromwell one of my words, the which he must want, seeing that he hath never kept any of his own.

Item: I give up the ghost.

∗

In his book *Country Lawyer*, Bellamy Partridge tells of the experience of his attorney father, Samuel Selden Partridge, in drawing a will for a client, Kate Vandenberg. ("Everybody in town knew what she was, though of course some of the men knew better than others.")

For years Kate was harassed by an ardent reformer who swore he would put her out of business. In fact, he ran for village president on a platform that stressed ridding the town of vice in general—and Kate in particular. He never had the opportunity to make good on his promise, for shortly after he was elected, Kate died.

Kate left a will and in it she left a modest sum of money "to one who had long been her valued friend"— the village president!

✳

This fifth day of May,
Being airy and gay,
To trip not inclined,
But of vigorous mind,
And my body in health,
I'll dispose of my wealth;
And of all I'm to leave
On this side the grave,
To some one or other,
I think to my brother.

But because I presaw
That my brothers-in-law
I did not take care,
Would come in for a share,
Which I noways intended,
Till their manners were mended—
And of that there's no sign.

I do therefore enjoin,
And strictly command,
As witness my hand,
That nought I have got
Be brought to hotch-pot.

And I give and devise,
Much as in me lies,
To the son of my mother,
My own dear brother,
To have and to hold
All my silver and gold,
As th' affectionate pledges
Of his brother,

JOHN HEDGES

This will in verse was proved in an English court in the year 1737.

"He makes out a new will every week. Says he never had so much fun in his life."

Courtesy Al Kaufman

Vindictive Wills

The Last Will and Testament of Herman Oberweiss, offered for probate in Texas, in June of 1934.

I am writing of my will mineself that des lawyir want he should have to much money he ask to many answers about the family. First think i dont want my brother Oscar to get a god dam thing i got he is a mumser and he done me out of four dollars fourteen years since.

I want it that Hilda my sister she gets the north sixtie akers of at where i am homing at now i bet she dont get that loafer husband of hers to brake twenty akers next plowing. She cant have it if lets Oscar live on it i want i should have it back if she does.

Tell mama that six hundret dollars she has been looking for ten years is berried from the bakhouse behind about ten feet down. She better let little Fredrick do the digging and count it when he comes up.

Mama should the rest get but i want it so that Adolph should tell her what not she should do so no more slick irishers sell her vaken cleaner they noise like hell and a broom dont cost so much.

I want it that mine brother Adolph be my executor and i want it that the judge should please make Adolph plenty bond put up and watch him like hell. Adolph is a good bisness man but only a dumpph would trust him with a busted pfennig.

Oscar don't nothing get. Tell Adolph he can have a hudret dollars if he prove to judge Oscar dont nothing get. That dam sure fix Oscar.

HERMAN OBERWEISS

—from *The Judicial Humorist,* edited by William L. Prosser, Little, Brown and Company, Boston, 1952.

Excerpts from the Last Will and Testament of the Marquis d'Aligre:

Article VII. I withdraw from N. A. ——— and N——— the sum I had left them by a former will; they have so often proclaimed that I am a man who would cut a farthing in four, that I would on no account oblige them to change their opinion. . . .

Article X. I leave 20,000 francs a year to the invalids who being on guard on the Pont des Arts in 1839, and judging from the shabbiness of my dress that I was in distress, paid for me the five centimes toll. . . .

Article XIV. I leave 200,000 francs a year to the "Phalansterians"; but they are only to receive this sum on the day on which they shall have transformed the ocean into orangeade. . . .

Article XVI. Taking compassion on the poor of the first arrondissement, I desire that the value of the cereals harvested on my land at the next harvest shall be distributed to them in its entirety. . . .

Article XX. Finally, I leave to my relatives, oblivion; to my friends, ingratitude; to God, my soul. As for my body, it belongs to my family vault. . . .

The Marquis concludes his will with this message to his family:

As for you, my relatives, who have been so long spelling upon this fortune, on which "I had concentrated all my affections," you are not going to touch a penny of it, and not one of you will be able to boast that you have squandered the millions which the old Marquis d'Aligre had taken so many years to hoard up.

∗

"*The way everything has gone up, he might at least have cut us off with five dollars!*"

Drawing by Tobey

*

Edward Wortley Montagu, son of the English ambassador to Turkey, signed and executed in 1716 a curious will, which was published with some important names merely hinted at. It reads, in part:

. . . to my noble and worthy relation, the Earl of ———: I do not give his lordship any further part of my property because the best part of that he has contrived to take already.

Item. To Lord ———, I give nothing, because I know he'll bestow it on the poor.

Item. To ———, the author, for putting me in his travels, I give five shillings for his wit, undeterred by the charge of extravagance, since friends who have read his book consider five shillings too much.

Item. To Sir Robert Walpole I leave my political opinions, never doubting he can well *turn* them into cash, who has always found such an excellent market in which to *change* his own.

Item. My cast-off habit of swearing oaths I give to Sir Leopold D——, in consideration that no oaths have ever been able to find him yet.

*

IN THE NAME OF GOD, AMEN:

I, William Dunlop, of Gairbraid, in the township of Colburne, county and district of Huron, Western Canada, Esquire, being in sound health of body, and my mind just as usual (which my friends who flatter me say is no great shakes at the best of times), do make this my last will and testament as follows, revoking of course all former wills.

I leave the property of Gairbraid and all other landed property I may die possessed of to my sisters, Helen Boyle Story and Elizabeth Boyle Dunlop, the former because she is married to a minister whom (God help him) she henpecks; the latter because she is married to nobody nor is she like to be, for she is an old maid and not market rife. . . .

I leave my silver tankard to the eldest son of Old John, as the representative of the family. I would have left it to Old John himself, but he would melt it down and make temperance medals and that would be sacrilege.

I leave Parson Chavasse (Maggy's husband) the snuff box I got from the Sarnia Militia, as a small token of my gratitude for the service he has done the family in taking a sister that no man of taste would have taken.

I also give my late brother's watch to my brother Sandy, exhorting him at the same time to give up whiggery, radicalism and all other sins that do most beset him.

I leave John Caddle a silver tea-pot, the end that he may drink tea therefrom and comfort him under the affliction of a slatternly wife.

I leave my brother Alan my big silver snuff box, as I am informed he is rather a decent Christian with a swag belly and a jolly face. . . .

(signed) W. DUNLOP
August 31, 1842

Garvey B. White died in 1908. In his will he directed:

. . . that before anything else is done fifty cents be paid to my son-in-law to enable him to buy for himself a good stout rope with which to hang himself, and thus rid mankind of one of the most infamous scoundrels that ever roamed this broad land or dwelt outside of a penitentiary.

A Variety of Parchments

He may make a will upon his nail for anything he has to give.

OLD PROVERB

Mr. Meeson's Will, a novel by Rider Haggard, tells of a will tattooed on the back of the lovely heroine. This of course was fiction, and even Rider Haggard fans found it difficult to accept the fantastic tale. But in the following pages truth comes up with some tall stories of its own.

Included among the "strange parchments" admitted to probate in the United States were a will written on the back of a bridge score card (Mrs. Charlotte N. Lawrence of Hempstead, New York), a will written on the back of a visiting card (Theodore G. Harris) and a will written on a prescription blank (Dr. John H. Locke). M.

Grant Hawkins, a Philadelphia resident who died insolvent, wrote his will on the back of a dunning letter from a creditor.

*

A will probated in 1955 was written on a hatbox by a factory worker. In it he left everything to his common-law wife—"my only friend."

*

Otto G. Richter, who died in 1960, disposed of six million dollars by a will scrawled on a hospital chart.

*

The will of Frank C. Likas, probated April 26, 1955, was written on a paper doily at a table in an Oak Lawn, Illinois restaurant.

*

Mrs. Chleo Newman jotted down her will on the back of an envelope before starting off on an airplane trip in 1947. She wrote it in an airport restaurant before taking off (it was witnessed by a waitress) because "she had a premonition of disaster." The plane crashed over West Virginia, killing eighteen passengers, including Mrs. Newman.

*

Andrew Komlody's will, leaving all he possessed to his wife, was written in indelible pencil on the whitewashed wall of the Carteret, New Jersey, jail cell where he hung himself with strips made from his blanket. (It was Mrs. Komlody who had caused the arrest because, she said, her husband was jealous and making trouble.)

Mrs. Beth A. Baer, a blind woman, wrote out her will with a pen that ran out of ink. Handwriting expert Clark Sellers was able to make out the words from the indentations left on the paper by the pen. Mrs. Baer's "blank paper" will was filed for probate in the Los Angeles Superior Court on April 11, 1950.

The twenty-nine-word will of William Harold Taylor, probated in 1935, was written on the reverse side of a dance invitation. Some years before his death, as Mr. Taylor was setting out for Europe, a guest at his bon voyage party asked him if he had a will. Mr. Taylor drew the dance invitation from his pocket and wrote the will.

Mrs. Lorolina Nordquist, seventy-two, believing she was lost in the woods, wrote her will in green chalk on the wall of a shack where she sought shelter. Searchers found her will and located the unconscious woman on a mound of straw inside the shack. She later recovered.

"*In view of my firm belief in reincarnation, I do hereby direct that my entire estate be held in trust, pending my return to this earth.*"

56

In a world which seems sometimes to be drowning in paper, it is difficult to visualize the lack of a piece of paper when it is crucially needed. But, according to Lillian Pelkey and Madeline Higgins, nurses for the late George W. Hazeltine, such was the case when their dying patient suddenly decided to write his last will not too long ago.

Faced with a willing testator and a temporary paper shortage, the resourceful Miss Pelkey rose to the occasion. She pulled up her dress and offered Mr. Hazeltine a portion of her white petticoat on which to write his will—the bulk of his estate to a grandniece and ten thousand dollars each to Miss Pelkey and Miss Higgins as a reward for their devotion. Both women signed as witnesses.

"The Petticoat Will" was filed for probate in a Los Angeles court and the trial that ensued to determine the validity of the nurses' claim attracted national attention. The jury declared the will genuine but the judge ruled that it was null and void on a technicality: An individual named in a will cannot also act as a witness.

Entered for probate in 1913 and now residing with the register of wills, Philadelphia, Pennsylvania, is a page from a handwritten recipe book containing the will of Maggie Nothe.

Under the heading "Chili Sauce Without Working" appears the following:

4 quarts of ripe tomatoes, 4 small onions, 4 green peppers, 2 teacups of sugar, 2 quarts of cider vinegar, 2 ounces ground allspice, 2 ounces cloves, 2 ounces cinnamon, 12 teaspoonfuls salt. Chop tomatoes, onions and peppers fine, add the rest mixed together and bottle cold. Measure tomatoes when peeled. In case I die before my husband I leave everything to him.

(signed) MAGGIE NOTHE

*

Into the solemn atmosphere of an English court marched Maggie Barnes, widow of James Barnes, a canal pilot. In her hand she held an empty eggshell; on it was written with an indelible pencil in her husband's hand: "Jan. 1925. Mag. Everything I Possess. J.B."

This, claimed Maggie, was her husband's real Last Will, not the 1920 document which required that she share her late husband's eight-thousand-pound legacy with two stepsons.

When it was pointed out that an eggshell was a strange place for a will—and an unwitnessed will at that! —Maggie's attorney countered that this "document" should be considered a sailor's will executed at sea and therefore no witnesses were necessary.

Was this eggshell, inscribed by a canal boat pilot on the Manchester to Liverpool run, a "testamentary disposition by a mariner at sea"? Lord Marivale, surrogate of the Probate Court, Manchester, ruled against the egg-shell "will" and in favor of the earlier bequest written on a respectable sheet of paper and witnessed by three upstanding citizens.

∗

Mine detectors, clairvoyants, a talking parakeet and an ocean-going bottle were all part of a frantic, fantastic search for a will that nobody was really sure ever existed. The prize was the fifteen-million-dollar estate of Daisy Alexander, the third daughter of sewing machine monarch Isaac Singer. Events following Mrs. Alexander's death in 1939 led from a stately mansion in London to a lonely beach five thousand miles away in San Francisco.

Although Mrs. Alexander promised her solicitor, Barry Cohen, that he would be generously provided for in the new will she had drawn, the only will found after her death was a thirty-year-old document which disposed of only a small portion of the vast estate to several distant relatives. Convinced that a later will existed and goaded by visions of a fifteen-million-dollar pot at the end of the rainbow, solicitor Cohen initiated a marathon search that would extend over several decades.

Following a fruitless exploration of Mrs. Alexander's Grosvernor Square mansion, a mine detector was moved in and a careful, painstaking probe made of every inch of the ceiling and walls in the hope of finding a safe or receptacle holding the missing document.

Newspaper accounts of the search brought in hundreds of suggestions—a woman from a Kentish county with a "vision," a real honest-to-goodness witch doctor, a cultist with a pendulum that stops when it locates the missing item—and finally, a full-fledged clairvoyant named Frederick Liston. Liston ran his fingers over a letter written by Mrs. Alexander and from "sympathetic vibrations" he received came up with some astonishingly accurate revelations of every phase of the dead woman's life—everything, that is, except the location of the elusive will.

One of the servants remembered that Mrs. Alexander spent many of her last days with a pet parakeet, Bob. According to the servants Bob was a fluent talker. The search party, with a covey of reporters at its heels, took off in pursuit of the bird who might be persuaded to drop a hint into Mr. Cohen's receptive ear. The bird was traced through three subsequent owners and when finally located was not only dead but ingloriously stuffed.

In 1947, on a deserted beach in San Francisco, Jack Wurm, an unemployed restaurant worker, picked up a bottle washed ashore by the tide. He broke the neck of the bottle, pulled out the scrap of paper inside and read:

To avoid confusion, I leave my entire estate to the lucky person who finds this bottle and to my attorney, Barry Cohen, share and share alike.

DAISY ALEXANDER
June 20, 1937

Daisy Alexander often threw bottles into the ocean wondering where they would go. When news of the find reached London, Daisy's friends said that putting a will in a bottle would be "just like her."

An expert on ocean currents testified that it would take a bottle approximately twelve years to make such a trip. Jack Wurm found the bottle eleven years and eight months after the date on the will.

Solicitor Cohen and his potential co-beneficiary Jack Wurm were, it would seem, close to the pot of gold at last—except for one important detail. To be honored in a British court a will must be witnessed, an embellishment sadly lacking in the scrap of paper washed ashore in San Francisco. The "will" is still floating through the courts, bobbing up now and again, but twenty-four years after Daisy Alexander's death, no settlement has been reached.

$*$

High up on a shelf, among hundreds of volumes of wills filed at the Surrogate Court in the District of Kerrobert, Canada, sits an unlikely "document"—a fender cut from a farm tractor. Its presence is explained by an accident that occurred at noon on June 8, 1948, when a tractor accidentally backed up, pinning George Harris beneath a disc apparatus he was adjusting. Mr. Harris' hands were free but the lower part of his leg was caught and bleeding profusely, making it impossible for him to free himself and reach help.

He was found in that position nine hours later and rushed to the hospital, where he died shortly after. One of the men examining the accident site a few days later noticed some writing scratched on the fender of Harris' tractor. It read:

In case I die in this mess, I leave all to the wife.

CECIL GEORGE HARRIS

Bits of fender were found on the knife in the dead man's pocket and it was obvious that he had used the knife to scratch the message while pinned beneath the machine. The fender was removed from the tractor, admitted to probate and filed with the registrar of wills as the Last Will and Testament of George Harris.

∗

Informed by his doctor that he had only hours to live, Charles S. Orrin, a British businessman, wrote out his will in shorthand. The stenographic characters were so perfectly executed that the court reporter was able to read the document with ease and the will was admitted to probate without delay on August 7, 1922.

∗

Richard Brinkley's method of will forgery was almost too simple—it was destined to fail. At the bedside of old and ailing Mrs. Johanna Blume, he produced a piece of paper: Would Mrs. Blume like to join a small congenial group on a brief picnic in the country? If so, would she sign here please?

Mrs. Blume was, of course, not signing a picnic roster but her own will, neatly written out and hidden above the fold. Successful thus far, Brinkley repeated the ruse with two of his neighbors, whose signatures would serve as "witnesses" on the will.

When, shortly after, old Mrs. Blume passed away and Brinkley claimed her house and an eight-hundred-pound bank account under the terms of the will, the curiously folded sheet of paper was viewed with suspicion. Brinkley began to worry about what the witnesses would say. Having quickly concluded that their testimony could be troublesome, he resolved to get rid of the witnesses.

He called on the first witness, a Mr. Parket, and brought along a little gift—a bottle of oatmeal stout highly recommended for its restorative qualities. Mr. Parket never got to taste the stout, but his landlord, Richard Beck, and Beck's wife Elizabeth sneaked a large swallow while Parket was out of his room. Within minutes husband and wife died of convulsions from the effects of poisoning by prussic acid.

"Well, I'm sugared. That's very awkward, isn't it?" said Mr. Brinkley when he was arrested. Sugared he may have been, but hanged he was too—at Wardsworth Prison in England on August 13, 1907.

✳

"Now go out and get me a dog named Rover!"

Courtesy Larry Barth

Any listing of strange will "parchments" must include the nonexistent parchment of Edward P. McNulty, entered to probate by Surrogate Wingate of Kings County, New York, on February 21, 1923.

Because the actual will had been torn up and thrown away by mistake by a nurse shortly after the death of the testator, Mrs. McNulty's brother, Martin Malone, entered the witness stand and described the contents of the will disposing of one hundred thousand dollars in real and personal property. (To do this he had to waive his right as a beneficiary.) Surrogate Wingate ruled that there had been a will and that the contents were as alleged.

*

The female sex, noted for its long goodbys, will not easily upset the all-time world's record set by the late Mrs. Frederick Cook, the widow of a London drapery manufacturer. Her will, the longest on record, was admitted to probate on November 7, 1925. Its 95,940 words and 1,066 pages are contained in four bulky volumes (at 1925 prices, a copy of the will cost four hundred dollars).

Mrs. Cook left an estate valued at one hundred thousand dollars with instructions that her diary be burned and, once again reverting to womanly ways, a request that her age be omitted from the memorial stone.

*

The briefest, smallest will on record was written on the identification disc of a British soldier lost at sea. The complete text consisted of three words: "All to mother." It was scratched on the metal in characters so small that a microscope was needed to read the message.

Conditional Wills

A will is wealth's last caprice.

EDWARD BULWER-LYTTON

To a man accustomed to purchasing obedience for cash the mere incidence of his death need not be a handicap. Not as long as he can write a will setting forth the conditions that must be met or the benefits withheld. Projecting his authority beyond the grave, the will-maker gets a final chance to pay the piper and call the tune.

For example, a rector of a Yorkshire parish, who died in 1804 (roughly 150 years before the advent of the bikini), left a substantial sum to his daughter with this proviso:

Seeing that my daughter Anna has not availed herself of my advice touching the objectionable practice of going about with her arms bare up to the elbows, my will is that, should she continue after my death in this violation of the modesty of her sex, all the goods, chattels, moneys, land, and other that I have devised to her for the maintenance of her future life shall pass to the oldest of the sons of my sister Caroline.

Should anyone take exception to this my wish as being too severe, I answer that license in dress in a woman is a mark of a depraved mind.

The way the rector felt about bare arms, James Fleming felt about mustaches. Mr. Fleming, the owner of a large and thriving furniture factory, was a charitable man, a man who didn't have very strong feelings about any-thing—except mustaches, the sight of which he despised.

When he died in 1869, he left a will stipulating that each man in his employ was to receive ten pounds, pro-viding he did not wear a mustache. Being a generous man, he could not bring himself to cut off his mustached employees without a cent. They were to receive five pounds each.

A Californian named John Quincy Murray, who died in 1929, gave three thousand dollars to two granddaughters on condition that they give up bobbed hair, rouge and powder, jewelry, dances and movies, and that they wear their dresses "long at both ends."

He also left a thousand dollars to his grandson pro-vided he would forgo dances and motion pictures and that he would never grow a mustache.

"*If a way to take it with you is ever discovered, he reserves the right to come back for his.*"

Courtesy Charles Skiles
and the *Saturday Evening Post*

Obviously, it is not possible to be passive about mustaches. You either like them or you don't. Henry Budd, a prosperous shipbuilder who died in 1862, was another who didn't like mustaches and said so in his will:

In case my son Edward shall wear a mustache, then the devise hereinbefore contained in favor of him, his appointees, heirs and assigns of my said estate, called Pepper Park, shall be void; and I devise the same estate to my son William, his appointees, heirs and assigns. And in case my son William shall wear a mustache, then the devise hereinbefore contained in favor of him, his appointees, heirs, assigns of my said estate called Twickinham Park, shall be void; and I devise the said estate to my son Edward, his appointees, heirs and assigns. And in case my son Edward . . .

A Vienna banker making a large bequest of property and cash to his nephew stipulated that "he shall never, on any occasion, read a newspaper, his favorite occupation."

Nephews seem to be the favorite target of capricious millionaires. An exceedingly wealthy Englishman named Sergeant, who died without sons, left each of his nephews sizeable annuities, with a string attached:

As my nephews are fond of indulging themselves in bed in the morning, and as I wish them to prove to the satisfaction of my executors that they have got out of bed in the morning, and either employed themselves in business or taken exercise in the open air, from five to eight o'clock every morning from the fifth of April to the tenth of October, being three hours each day, and from seven to nine o'clock in the morning from the tenth of October to the fifth of April, being two hours every morning; this is to be done for some years, during the first seven years to the satisfaction of my executors, who may excuse them in case of illness, but the task must be made up when they are well, and if they will not do this, they shall not receive any share of my property. Temperance makes the faculties clear, and exercise makes them vigorous.

When he died in 1933, John D. Morgan of Elizabeth, New Jersey, left two million dollars but took with him the financial acumen that built so vast an estate. In recognition of this fact, Mr. Morgan stipulated in his will that his two daughters must first pass an examination on the "principles of sound investment" in order to qualify for the bequest. The will states that:

. . . they each thoroughly satisfy the trustees that they understand the principles of sound investment substantially as they are explained in some standard authoritative work on this subject; this examination must show that they have a practical knowledge of such principles, permanently understood and remembered, and not a mere temporary committing to memory of some book.

When he died in 1953, McNair Ilgenfritz left the Metropolitan Opera $150,000, the score for an opera that he composed and the condition that if the Met wanted the money it must also take the opera.

For a while it looked as if Mr. Ilgenfritz would realize posthumously a goal that eluded him during his lifetime. The bequest came at a time when the Metropolitan was having more than its usual financial problems, and serious consideration was given to accepting the conditions set forth in the will and presenting the late composer's work at the revered opera house. In the midst of mounting criticism that art was being compromised and the institution "bought off," the bequest was refused.

Mr. Ilgenfritz's opera was never produced at the Metropolitan Opera.

*

" . . . and to my sister, Emma Bentley, who often said she would bet a hundred dollars that a bunch of chorus girls would get my money, I leave one hundred dollars."

Courtesy Hank Ketcham

In 1957, Mrs. Viola Laski was left an inheritance of $325,000. According to the conditions of her mother's will she must live in the U.S. or be "physically present" at the quarterly distribution of interest.

Said British subject Mrs. Laski: "I shall forgo the money."

Husbands and Wives

*The comfortable estate of widowhood is the only hope
that keeps up a wife's spirits.*

JOHN GAY, *The Beggar's Opera*

A French merchant who died in the year 1610 left a handsome legacy to a lady who had refused to marry him twenty years before. He did so, he said in his will, to express his gratitude for "a happy bachelor life of independence and freedom."

Not everyone is that fortunate. Instead of a rejection many a man has found himself a short-term winner and a long-term loser: she said "yes" and he lived unhappily ever after. Then, after years of misery, the aggrieved husband finds, at last, the perfect device with which to strike back. Through his will he hopes to have the last word even if it means reaching out from beyond the grave to do so.

Such a man was John Packer, a wealthy bookseller

living at Old Bond Street, London until his death in 1791.

To one Elizabeth Packer, whom through fondness I made my wife, without regard to family, fame and fortune, and who in return has not spared most unjustly to accuse me of every crime regarding human nature, except highway robbery, I bequeath fifty pounds.

"I am reading it right. He left his money to Johns Hopkins and his brain to you!"

Courtesy Bo Brown

Excerpt from the will of Henry, Earl of Stafford (seventeenth century):

I give to the worst of women, who is guilty of all ills—the daughter of Mr. Gramont, a Frenchman—whom I have unfortunately married, five and forty brass halfpence, which will buy her a pullet for her supper—a greater sum than her father can often make over to her—for I have known when he had neither money nor credit for such a purchase, he being the worst of men, and his wife the worst of women in all debaucheries.

Colonel Charles Nash, who died at the end of the nineteenth century, bequeathed an annuity of fifty pounds to the bell ringers of Bath Abbey, England, on the condition that they muffle the clappers of the bells and "ring them with doleful accentuation" from 8 A.M. to 8 P.M. on each anniversary of his wedding day and, during the same hours, "with a merry peal" on the anniversary of the day in which death released him from the tyranny of domestic togetherness.

John George of Lambeth died in London in June 1791. His wife not only drove him to distraction but to the heights of eloquence:

Seeing that I have had the misfortune to be married to the aforesaid Elizabeth, who, ever since our union, has tormented me in every possible way; that not content with making game of all my remonstrances, she has had done all she could to render my life miserable; that Heaven seems to have sent her into the world solely to drive me out of it; that the strength of Samson, the genius of Homer, the prudence of Augustus, the skill of Pyrrhus, the patience of Job, the philosophy of Socrates, the subtlety of Hannibal, the vigilance of Hermogenes, would not suffice to subdue the perversity of her character; that no power on earth can change her, seeing we have lived apart during the last eight years, and that the only result has been the ruin of my son, whom she has corrupted and estranged from me; weighing maturely and seriously all these considerations, I have bequeathed, and I bequeath, to my said wife Elizabeth, the sum of one shilling, to be paid unto her within six months of my death.

∗

What other men before and after him have tried to say, an anonymous New Jersey testator said with less words and more art. Until a better one comes to light, it remains the epitome of succinct vituperation:

"To my wife Anna (who is no damn good) I leave $1."

∗

Many men will find a bold champion in the person of William Durley. His will, filed in the nineteenth century, reads:

To my wife, Mary, one shilling, in recompence of her having picked my pocket of sixty guineas, and taken up money in my name, without my leave or license.

Mr. Durley's countryman John Davis cut his wife off with five shillings:

It is sufficient to enable her to get drunk for the last time at my expense.

Angry husbands may sympathize with these avenged testators of yesteryear but it is not possible for them to do likewise. The laws of all the states in the U.S., Great Britain and many other countries set a minimum share of the estate which a widow is entitled to if she contests the will and claims her "dower rights."

Any schoolboy can repeat Patrick Henry's stirring "give me liberty or give me death," but few people indeed are aware of the patriot's attitude on widow's rights. After making generous provisions in his will for his wife and children, Patrick Henry declares:

But in case my said wife shall marry again, in that case I revoke and make void every gift, legacy, authority, or power herein mentioned and order, will and direct, She, my said Wife, shall have no more of my estate than she can recover by Law; nor shall she be Guardian to any of my children, or Executrix of this my Will.

Like her late husband, Dorothea Henry counted freedom of action above security. Disregarding the penalty, she remarried, taking as her new spouse Judge Edmund Winston, who was Patrick Henry's cousin.

Late in life, Gouverneur Morris, the celebrated orator and New York statesman, married Miss Ann Randolph, a lady much younger than himself. In appreciation of their short, happy life together, Gouverneur Morris bequeathed a handsome income to his young widow, providing in his will that in the event that she remarried the income should be doubled.

∗

The German poet Heinrich Heine left a will giving his wife all his assets, with one condition—that she remarry. "Because," he says in his will, "then there will be at least one man to regret my death."

∗

When André Fraysse found himself a widower at the tender age of twenty-three he was distraught. When he learned soon after that his wife had bequeathed a small fortune for use other than his own he was inconsolable.

On August 9, 1925, he and his mother presented themselves at the office of the local notary to argue the point. Having failed to convince the notary that the recently deceased wife was insane at the time the will was drawn, mother and son resorted to extreme methods. Mme. Fraysse snatched the will and as the notary hurled upon her to recover the document she passed it quickly to her son. Then, in the words of *The New York Times* account of the incident, "The latter quickly put it into his mouth, chewed it violently and swallowed it without a pause, before the eyes of the astonished notary."

Unfortunately for M. Fraysse, this gastronomic feat went unrewarded. A carbon copy of the will just as effectively cut him off without a franc.

"You're missing a lot of fun by sticking to one will!"
Drawing by Skiles

In one of the most remarkable bequests on record, Mrs. Robert C. Hayes, of Binghamton, New York, left her husband Robert—a new wife. The bride was Annamae, Mrs. Hayes' eldest daughter by a previous marriage.

The testator, who died in December of 1920, sought in a single stroke to promote the future happiness of her young husband and her divorced daughter. She left instructions that the two were to be married after her death and that the marriage ceremony was to take place within five days of her funeral.

Mrs. Hayes was buried on Wednesday. The following Monday, the recently widowed Robert Hayes, thirty-five, and his stepdaughter Annamae, twenty-one, were married.

*

It was Mormon leader Brigham Young's rare experience to write a will for the distribution of his estate among seventeen wives and forty-eight children. The will, disposing of two and a half million dollars in cash and property, divides the families into "classes," each class being represented by a wife and children, or a wife without children or the children of a deceased wife. The Mormon prophet was also "sealed" to a number of other women, in accordance with the ritual of the Mormon Church, but there is no accurate count of this category and no mention is made of them in his will. Brigham Young drew on his considerable experience in the subject and stated in his will just what he meant by "a wife":

To avoid any question, the words *married* or *marriage* in this will shall be taken to have become consummated between man and woman, either by ceremony before a lawful magistrate or according to the order of the Church of Jesus Christ of Latter-Day Saints, or by their cohabitation in conformity to our custom.

∗

The three-page will of William Shakespeare—probably the most famous will in existence—is preserved in an airtight frame of thick glass and polished oak. This priceless document is kept in Somerset House, London, along with the wills of such luminaries as Samuel Johnson, Lord Nelson, William Pitt, Isaak Walton, the Duke of Wellington and John Milton.

Within the formal, legalistic language of Shakespeare's will, one provocative line catches the eye of the curious reader: "Item: I give unto my wife my second best bed . . ."

Is this confirmation of an unhappy married life—or a sentimental bequest motivated by love?

Many scholars and historians explain that "the second best bed" was the one associated with the couple's domestic life and so, rather than a personal slight, it was a romantic, thoughtful bequest. Others are not so sure. They point out that it was the custom during Shakespeare's time for men to mention their wives in their wills with high praise and terms of endearment. Not only was this missing in the Bard's will but even the modest bequest of the "second best bed" was an interlineation—an afterthought hastily scribbled in.

Those who look to Shakespeare's will to provide clues to the true relationship between Anne Hathaway and

William Shakespeare must conclude that it only adds to the mystery.

"As executor of the will—"

Drawing by Ben Roth

Curiosities of the Search Room, a book published in England in 1880, records this nineteenth-century will:

> As to all my worldly goods now, or to be, in store,
> I give to my beloved wife, and hers for evermore.
> I give all freely, I no limit fix:
> This is my will, and she's executrix.

Unlike the poet who conceived it, this bit of verse has many lives. The same will, word for word, was admitted to probate in Newark on May 13, 1921 (Frederick E. Castle), in Bronx County on May 30, 1925 (Morris Deitsch) and twenty-one years later, on May 16, 1946, in Edgar County Court (John W. Maughmer). It is unlikely that collectors of odd wills have seen the last of it.

A Sense of History

The tongues of dying men
Enforce attention like deep harmony . . .

SHAKESPEARE, *Richard II*

While directing the excavations at Kahun, British archeologist Sir William Petrie unearthed a bit of papyrus folded vertically and sealed with a scarabaeus, a large black beetle regarded by ancient Egyptians as symbolic of resurrection and immortality. Translation by an Oxford scholar revealed the Last Will of Uah, dating back to some time around 1799 B.C. The will is a model of simplicity and clarity.

I, Uah, am giving a title to property to my wife Sheftu, the woman of Gesab who is called Teta, the daughter of Sat Sepdu, of all things given to me by my brother Ankh-ren.

85

She shall give it to any she desires of her children she bears me.

I am giving to her the Eastern slaves, four persons, that my brother Ankh-ren gave me. She shall give them to whomsoever she will of her children.

As to my tomb, let me be buried in it with my wife alone.

Moreover, as to the house built for me by my brother, Ankh-ren, my wife shall dwell therein without allowing her to be put forth on the ground by any person.

Done in the presence of these witnesses. Kemen, decorator of columns. Apu, doorkeeper of the Temple. Senb, son of Senb, doorkeeper of the Temple.

King's son Nek'ure makes the following command while living upon his two feet and not ailing in any respect.

The remainder of this will, carved on the wall of a tomb some time around the year 2601 B.C., is barely decipherable. In it, Nek'ure, son of the pharaoh King Khafre, disposes of fourteen towns and two estates in the pyramid city created by his father. The property was to be divided among his wife, three children and an unknown person, possibly his mistress.

Fragments of the carving containing Nek'ure's will, the oldest known to exist, can be found in the Berlin Museum.

The oldest will in the United States is filed at the courthouse in Lancaster County, Virginia. It is the will of

Epraphrodibus Lawson of Rappahannock, Virginia, dated March 31, 1652.

*

South African empire-builder Cecil Rhodes was obsessed with wills. The first of his six wills, written when he was a twenty-four-year-old undergraduate at Oxford, set the theme that he would return to again and again:

. . . to and for the establishment, promotion and development of a Secret Society, the true aim and object whereof shall be the extension of British rule throughout the world, . . . the ultimate recovery of the United States of America as an integral part of the British Empire . . . and, finally, the foundation of so great a Power as hereafter to render wars impossible and promote the best interest of humanity.

The next four wills contained variations of the Rhodesian manifesto for British domination of the world. However, when he drafted his sixth and last will, Rhodes perhaps sensed that this was to be the one that mattered, for he put aside his grandiose schemes and settled for reality. The essence of the will, as the world knows it, is the section which created the famous Rhodes Scholarships.

In the person of the Rhodes Scholar, a young man from either Britain, the U.S. or Germany, lies Cecil Rhodes' hope of Anglo-Saxon supremacy in the world.

With these words, Alfred Nobel, inventor of dynamite and nitroglycerine, established the most important prizes for achievement, the most sought-after distinction, anywhere in the world:

The whole of my remaining estate shall be dealt with in the following way: The capital shall be invested by my executors in safe securities and shall constitute a fund, the interest on which shall be annually distributed in the form of prizes to those who, during the preceding year, shall have conferred the greatest benefit on mankind.

The said interest shall be divided into five parts, which shall be apportioned as follows: one part to the person who shall have made the most important discovery or invention within the field of physics; one part to the person who shall have made the most important chemical discovery or improvement; one part to the person who shall have made the most important discovery within the domain of physiology or medicine; one part to the person who shall have produced in the field of literature the most outstanding work of an idealistic tendency; and one part to the person who shall have done the most or the best work for fraternity among nations, for the abolition or reduction of standing armies and for the holding and promotion of peace congresses.

.   .   .   .

It is my express wish that in awarding the prizes no consideration whatever shall be given to the nationality of the candidate, so that the most worthy shall receive the prize whether he be a Scandinavian or not.

Paris, November 27, 1895   ALFRED BERNHARD NOBEL

Events since the first Nobel Peace Prize was awarded provide an ironic footnote to Nobel's Last Will and

Testament. The awards were continued all through the First World War but in 1940 they were suspended as the world waged the greatest war in history. The factories on both sides that fed ammunition to the conflicting forces were descendants of the original Nobel Explosive Company. The prizes were restored in 1943.

*

The will of Peter I (Czar of Russia from 1696 to 1725) presents a blueprint for the Russian domination of Europe. Although written more than two centuries ago, it has a familiar ring:

God, from whom we derive our existence, and to whom we owe our crown, having constantly enlightened us by his Spirit, and sustained us by his divine help, allows me to look on the Russian people as called upon hereafter *to hold sway over Europe!*

My reason for thus thinking is that the European nations have mostly reached a state of old age, bordering on imbecility, or they are rapidly approaching it; naturally, then, they will be easily and *indubitably* conquered by a people strong in youth and vigor, especially when this latter shall have attained its full strength and power. I look on the future invasion of the eastern and western countries by the north as a periodical movement, ordained by Providence, who in like manner regenerated the Roman nation barbarian invasions. . . .

I found Russia as a *rivulet:* I leave it a *river;* my successors will make it a *large sea,* destined to fertilize the impoverished lands of Europe; and its waters will overflow, in spite of opposing dams, erected by weak hands, if our descendants only know how to direct its course. This is the reason I leave the following instructions:

I. Keep the Russian nation in a *state of continual war*, so as to have the soldier always under arms, and ready for action, excepting when the finances of the state will not allow it. Keep up the forces; choose the best moment for attack. By this means you will be ready for war even in the time of peace. This is for the interest of the future aggrandizement of Russia.

II. Endeavor, by every possible means, to bring in, from the neighboring civilized countries of Europe, officers in times of war, and learned men in times of peace, thus giving the Russian people the advantages enjoyed by other countries, without allowing them to lose any of their own self-respect.

III. On every occasion take a part in the affairs and quarrels of Europe: above all, in . . . Germany . . .

The above, followed by a detailed plan of strategy, constitutes the Last Will and Testament of Peter the Great. Seven years after it was written George Washington was born.

From the Last Will and Testament of Napoleon, written on April 15, 1821 at St. Helena, the first five items:

1. I die in the apostolical Roman religion, in the bosom of which I was born, more than fifty years since.

2. It is my wish that my ashes may repose on the banks of the Seine, in the midst of the French people, whom I have loved so well.

3. I have always had reason to be pleased with my dearest wife, Marie Louise. I retain for her to my last moment, the most tender sentiments—I beseech her to watch, in order to preserve my son from the snares which yet environ his infancy.

4. I recommend to my son, never to forget that he was born a French prince, and never to allow himself to become an instrument in the hands of the triumvirs who oppress the nations of Europe; he ought never to fight against France, or to injure her in any manner; he ought to adopt my motto—"Everything for the French people."

5. I die prematurely, assassinated by the English oligarchy. . . . The English nation will not be slow in avenging me.

✳

The Case of Myra Gaines Clark is by all odds the most remarkable case involving a will ever to be tried in American courts. The struggle to capture the thirty-million-dollar estate of Daniel Clark raged in the law courts for fifty years, appearing on ten separate occasions before the United States Supreme Court. Among the thirty lawyers who worked on the case were such luminaries as Daniel Webster, Reverdy Johnson and Francis Scott Key.

When Daniel Clark died in 1825, a will was filed which left the estate to Clark's elderly mother. Myra Gaines, his daughter, claimed that this will was fraudulent, that her father wrote a later will in 1813 leaving the estate to her.

Where was the 1813 will? According to Mrs. Gaines, it

had been lost, stolen or destroyed—but, said she, such a will did at one time exist and she had a witness who had read it while her father was still alive.

Mrs. Gaines had to prove more than the existence of a will: She had to prove that, contrary to general belief, her parents were legally married. Unless she could prove her own legitimacy she could not inherit in Louisiana, where the Roman Code system of law is in force.

Although the fortune was vast, more than money was at stake. Mrs. Gaines was fighting for her mother's honor and for her own good name and it was this element of the case that captured the sympathy and interest of millions. Through fifty tempestuous years of American history, the slight figure of a woman pitted against impossible odds never left the public scene.

Defeated in New Orleans, Mrs. Gaines pressed her case in the federal courts. Defeated in the Supreme Court, Mrs. Gaines hired a new lawyer and began again. Forty years after her father's death, the Supreme Court acknowledged the existence of the will and accepted the testimony that a marriage did take place. The case was won but the benefits were still unrealized. It was 1864 and the nation was split in two by the Civil War. According to the rules of the confederacy, "any judgment rendered by a court of the United States shall be null and void in any seceded state."

After the war the legal cudgels were picked up and victory came once again, but by then the potentially richest woman in the United States was too old to care and too tired to pursue her claim. On January 1, 1885, after half a century of fighting, Myra Gaines Clark, old and in debt, died in a poorly furnished upstairs rented room.

*

From the will of Benjamin Franklin:

To my son William Franklin, late Governor of the Jerseys, I give and devise all the lands I hold or have a right to in the Province of Nova Scotia, to hold to him, his heirs and assigns forever. I also give him all my books and papers which he has in his possession, and all debts standing against him on my account books, willing that no payment for restitution of the same be required of him by my Executors. The part he acted against me in the late war, which is of public notoriety, will account for my leaving him no more of an estate he endeavored to deprive me of.

In contrast to the bitterness displayed toward his son, Franklin showered gifts and affection on his daughter Sarah and her husband Richard Bache.

"I wish to be useful even after my Death, if possible," wrote Franklin, and to this end he left one thousand pounds each to the cities of Philadelphia and Boston to be loaned out to young artisans after they had served their apprenticeship. The apprenticeship system has all but vanished from the American scene and much of the money set aside for helping young apprentices to get started has been redirected. Many millions of dollars for charity and public works were generated by Franklin's original two-thousand-pound gift.

Franklin's will also includes this bequest:

My fine crabtree walking stick with a gold head, curiously wrought in the form of the cap of liberty, I give to my friend, and the friend of mankind, George Washington.

If it was a sceptre, he has merited and would become it.

We shall follow the walking stick with a gold head as it passes through the will of Washington.

∗

George Washington's lengthy will begins by disposing of his estate to Martha Washington ("my dearly beloved wife") and continues with this expression of Washington's wishes for the destiny of his slaves:

Upon the decease of my wife, it is my will and desire that all the Slaves which I hold in my own right shall receive their freedom. To emancipate them during her life, would, though earnestly wished by me, be attended with such *insufferable* difficulties on account of their intermixture by marriage with the dower Negroes, as to excite the most painful sensations . . . it not being in my power, under the tenure by which the dower Negroes are held, to manumit them.

And Whereas, among those who will receive freedom according to this devise, there may be some who from old age or bodily infirmities, and others who, on account of their infancy, that will be unable to support themselves, it is my will and desire that all who come under the first and second description, shall be comfortably clothed and fed by my heirs while they live; and that such of the latter description as have no parents living, or, if living, are unable or unwilling to provide for them, shall be bound by the court until they shall arrive at the age of twenty-five years. . . .

The Negroes thus bound are (by their masters or mistresses) to be taught to read & write & be bro't up to some useful occupation, agreeably to the laws of the commonwealth of Virginia, providing for the support of orphan and other poor children. . . .

And I do, moreover, most pointedly and most solemnly enjoin it upon my Executors hereafter named or the survivor of them to see that this clause respecting Slaves and every part thereof, be religiously fulfilled at the epoch at which it is directed to take place, without evasion, neglect, or delay, after the crops which may then be on the ground are harvested, particularly as it respects the aged and infirm. . . .

And to my mulatto man William (calling himself William Lee) I give immediate freedom, or if he should prefer it (on account of accidents which have befallen him and which have rendered him incapable of walking or of any active employment) to remain in the situation he now is, it shall be optional in him to do so; in either case, however, I allow him an annuity of Thirty Dollars during his natural life . . . and this I give him as a testimony of my sense of his attachment to me, and for his faithful services during the Revolutionary War. . . .

The "dower Negroes" referred to in the excerpt were the slaves owned by Martha. She claimed them as her dower right in her first marriage to Daniel Parke Custis. President Washington had only a life interest in them by reason of his marriage to the former Mrs. Custis.

Washington's request that his freed slaves "be taught to read & write" was never carried out. The laws of the

State of Virginia at that time expressly prohibited schools for the instruction of Negroes.

"My mulatto man William" served as Washington's attendant during the Revolutionary War until he was injured in battle and was unable to continue. William Lee grew quite famous after President Washington died and as the legend grew "William Lees" turned up everywhere. He had five different funerals—each reported as the funeral of the original William Lee. He died once in North Carolina, once in Missouri, once in Arkansas, twice in New York.

Among the personal bequests, the following item appears:

Item: To my brother, Charles Washington, I give and bequeath the Gold headed cane left me by Dr. Franklin in his will.

The cane that passed through two famous American wills is now the property of the United States government.

Millions left by a New Englander to establish a home for indigent sailors of whaling ships, another estate left for the benefit of wool carders in Massachusetts, a special fund set up to ransom American seamen held by pirates on the North African coast—these are just a few of the thousands of bequests destined to become curiosity items. The causes or persons they sought to help no longer exist and the testators' good intentions have been defeated by progress.

A famous case of this kind involves the estate of Bryan Mullanphy, a former mayor of St. Louis who died in 1851. In his will, Judge Mullanphy set aside $200,000

to constitute a fund to furnish relief to all poor emigrants and travelers coming to St. Louis on their way to settle the west.

As time passed it became more and more difficult to find emigrants on their way to settle the west. In 1934, living relatives of Mullanphy sought to dissolve the trust and acquire the assets, which, with interest added, was worth over a million dollars. The city of St. Louis opposed the dissolution, contending that it would be inconsistent with Judge Mullanphy's intent since he made no provision for any relatives in his will. The court found that "while the Sante Fe and the Oregon trails may be paved with concrete and poor travelers may be outfitted in Model T Fords rather than Prairie Schooners, there still must be poor travelers who need assistance."

Today even the Model T has passed from the scene, but in the St. Louis railroad station and bus depot are fully staffed offices ready to help anyone who needs assistance. The sign on the door reads, "Mullanphy Traveler's Aid."

"*My goodness! Your dear old uncle seems to have left everything to me.*"

Drawing by Peter Arno;
© 1942 The New Yorker Magazine, Inc.

Revelations

Truth sits upon the lips of dying men.

MATTHEW ARNOLD

Some testators give away more than their property—
they give themselves away. Rufus Hatch, for example.
Mr. Hatch, who departed this life in 1881, advised his
sons to learn a trade rather than a profession in order
that "they will always be sure of an honest living." He
added:

I earnestly desire that my children shall not gamble in any
way for money, as their father has had experience sufficient
for all posterity.

1.

2.

3.

4.

This is my last will,
I insist on it still;
To sneer on and welcome,
And e'en laugh your fill.

    I, William Hickington,
Poet of Pocklington,
Do give and bequeath,
As free as I breathe,
To thee, Mary Jarum
The Queen of my Harum,
My cash and my cattle,
With every chattel,
To have and to hold,
Come heat or come cold,
Sans hindrance or strife,
Though thou art not my wife.
As witness my hand,
Just here as I stand.
The twelfth of July
In the year Seventy.
             WM. HICKINGTON

William Hickington died in 1770. His rhyming will was admitted to probate at the Deanery Court in the City of York, England.

In lieu of cash, William Hampton, who died at the beginning of this century, left his son a copy of Lawrie's "Interest Tables." According to his will, this prudent Englishman did so

. . . not for its intrinsic value, but from the hope that so small an incident may be of use to him in future years. And I particularly recommend to him the study of the compound interest tables, as showing that from comparatively small investments, by patience, large sums may be realized.

"I'm afraid your uncle wasn't as wealthy as everyone thought."
Courtesy Richter
and the *Saturday Evening Post*

In a will written at the turn of the century, Joseph H. Melchior of Seattle disposed of $120,000 in particular and the legal profession in general:

I never liked lawyers as a class and to keep away from them and steer clear of their inveigling schemes and grasping machination—ever an active ingredient in their diabolical profession—has been my constant life-long effort. . . .

The incontrovertible facts in my case are these—there never was a better, all-round individual ever set foot upon the regions of this broad state than myself.

"What sort of will would you like to have, Mr. Fignewton? . . . Short and simple? . . . Or one that will go clear to the Supreme Court?"

Courtesy George Lichty,
and Field Enterprises, Inc.

The French attorney who wrote his will at about the same time as Mr. Melchior makes a stunning reply in the never-ending dialogue between lawyer and client.

The attorney's will reads:

I give 100,000 francs to the local madhouse. I obtained this money out of those who pass their lives in litigation; in bequeathing it for the use of lunatics I only make restitution.

John Randolph, the famous American statesman, was known throughout his life for his sharp, biting tongue. In the writing of his will, this peculiar talent did not forsake him.

As lawyers and courts of law are extremely addicted to making wills for dead men, which they never made when living, it is my will and desire that no person who shall set aside, or attempt to set aside, the will above referred to, shall ever inherit, possess, or enjoy any part of my estate. . . .

Isaac Norris of Philadelphia made this poetic admonition in his will, admitted to probate in 1735:

> He that perverts this will of mine
> View well this lot, 'twill soon be thine.
> Plain words, with obvious meaning, need no School
> In wills, the Intention is the rigorous Rule.

" . . . and thus, my ghoulish friends, ends the first chapter of my last will and testament. Be sure to listen again tomorrow. . . . Will Grace get her hooks on any of this money—she who often called me an old goat? . . . Who are the three characters, each destined to be cut off with one lousy dollar? . . . And my faithful wife, affectionately known as Old Howler—will she find that the state law on widow's rights, after all, could foil my clever lawyer and good friend? . . ."

Exit Laughing

Let the world slide, let the world go,
A fig for care, and a fig for woe!
If I can't pay, why I can owe,
And death makes equal the high and low.

Wayne Morris, the movie star, died in 1959 at the age of forty-five. A portion of his will reads:

One hundred dollars shall be expended at the discretion of my closest surviving relatives for the purpose of buying booze and canapés for my friends. On second thought make it three hundred dollars because I don't want my friends to go away sober or serious.

*

A case of bourbon went to J. Wesley Cupp, a Los Angeles lawyer, by the will of his friend, Edward P. Hadley, of San Diego, California, in August 1947, he to quaff the same at his leisure, not to extend over a period longer than necessary to consume the same in the presence and company of many other of my pals in Los Angeles.

✳

Jerry Hilborn has been dead for over twenty-five years but, according to the terms of his will, he has been the "host" at a dance held every year in his honor by the people of West Minot, Maine.

✳

In a will probated in London in 1946, George Lofcoate provided £208 for the boys at the neighborhood pub to drink his health "every Sunday at 1 P.M. as long as the money holds out." The same year, Louis Gardiol of California passed on, leaving instructions in his will "to set 'em up for the pallbearers" and twelve dollars to cover the tab. Immediately after the funeral the six pallbearers complied with Gardiol's last request.

✳

This lighthearted approach to a grim occasion is reminiscent of the frolic that took place in Padua on July 17, 1418. Well-documented accounts of the event tell of a joyous celebration, much more like a wedding than the funeral ceremony that it actually was. The festive atmosphere was the idea of the late Lodovico Cortusio, formerly Jurisconsultus of Padua, who spelled out carefully in his will each detail of his funeral. In accordance with the will, there was to be a feast and entertainment accompanied by "the sound of lutes, violins, hautboys, trumpets, tambourines and other musical instruments." Weeping by relatives or friends was absolutely forbidden and, as an incentive to merriment, an additional bequest was offered to the member of the funeral party who laughed most heartily.

Quite different—and yet, as it turned out, not so different —was the exit of a devout Italian spinster who died in the early part of the seventeenth century.

Shocked by the irreverence of the clergy during funeral ceremonies, she took special precautions to insure the solemnity of her own leave-taking. In a special clause in her will, she declared that if any priest so much as smiled or showed any signs of levity, he was to be excluded from sharing in the large bequest for the benefit of the clergymen present at the ceremony.

When, at the elderly woman's death, her brother explained the unusual clause to the assembled clergymen, they expressed shock at the implication. But once the procession was under way, the priests began to eye each other with a peculiar twinkle; the ban on frivolity was a difficult one to forget. The twinkle became a smirk, the smirk a grin, the grin a smile, and finally a laugh that spread infectiously among the priests until the ceremony collapsed under gales of laughter.

The brother refused to pay any of the fees and the affair was brought before the tribunal. According to old records of the dispute, the decision was made in favor of the clergy on the ground that "the absurdity of the prohibition was in itself a provocation to violate it."

"This is the Last Will and Testament of Elias M. Pinzer, dentist. This is going to hurt a little . . ."

Courtesy Henry Boltinoff
and *Woman's Home Companion*

"Back to reading of the will in just a minute, friends, but first, a word about our law firm, Linder, Hall, Smoot and Carver."

Courtesy Bill Yates
and the *Saturday Evening Post*

Among the bequests of Charles A. Murray, whose will was probated in Cumberland County, New Jersey, in 1908:

I give, bequeath and devise to Lyon Post G.A.R. the sum of twenty-five dollars to buy some fun, even if they have to jump the aquarium to get it; their time is getting short so they had better get a move on.

To all my other friends and relations I leave my blessing and the assurance that I will do all I can for them up here, as soon as I find out "where I am at."

John B. Kelly Sr.

A CLASSIC WILL

It is ironic that an individual as colorful and unique as Jack Kelly should be generally known and referred to as "Grace Kelly's father." He was a remarkable man who never required any reflection of glory. Long before his daughter Grace became a movie star and Her Serene Highness Princess Grace of Monaco, Jack Kelly achieved eminence, rising from bricklayer to millionaire contractor. With two minor exceptions, Mr. Kelly's widow, Margaret, three daughters and a son were made the sole beneficiaries of the will.

It is difficult to say whether this colorful Irishman's unique testament will encourage and inspire others to make their own will a personal document in addition to an instrument which transfers property. It will, I think, suggest the possibilities. Jack Kelly had something to say which would not fit into the mold of legal terminology, so he said it his way without endangering the validity of the will or the rights of his heirs.

In the selected clauses that follow, Mr. Kelly speaks for himself:

For years I have been reading Last Wills and Testaments, and I have never been able to clearly understand any of them at one reading. Therefore I will attempt to write my own will in the hope that it will be understandable and legal. Kids will be called "kids" and not "issue," and it will not be cluttered up with "parties of the first part," "per stirpes," "perpetuities," "quasi-judicial," "to wit," and a lot of other terms that I am sure are only used to confuse those for whose benefit it is written.

This is my Last Will and Testament and I believe I am of sound mind. (Some lawyers will question this when they read my Will; however, I have my opinion of some of them, so that makes it even.)

. . . .

Godfrey Ford has been with me over forty-five years, and has been a faithful and loyal servant. Therefore, I want him to be kept in employment as long as he behaves himself well, making due allowances for minor errors of the flesh, if being slightly on the Casanova side is an error. I want my survivors to feel an obligation regarding his comfort and employment. In addition, I give him $1,000 outright. I have already turned over to him the bonds I bought for him at Christmas each year. . . .

After providing for his daughters and son John, Kelly approaches the matter of his sons-in-law, among them Prince Rainier of Monaco:

In the case of my daughters' husbands, they do not share and if any of my daughters dies, her share goes to her children, or if there are no children, then that share goes back into my own children's fund. I don't want to give the impression that I am against sons-in-law—if they are the right type they will provide for themselves and their families and what I am able to give my daughters will help pay the dress shop bills, which, if they continue as they have started out, under the able tutelage of their mother, will be quite considerable. . . .

.   .   .   .

I can think of nothing more ghastly than the heirs sitting around listening to some representative reading a Will. They always remind me of buzzards and vultures awaiting the last breath of the stricken. Therefore, I will try to spare that ordeal and let you read the Will before I go to my reward—whatever it will be. I do hope that it will never be necessary to go into Court over spoils, for to me the all-time low in family affairs is a court fight, in which I have seen families engage. If you cannot agree, I will direct that the executor or trustees, as the case may be, shall decide all questions of administration or distribution, as the executor and trustees will be of my choosing or yours. . . .

I will try to give each of you all I can during my life so that you will have money in your own right—in that way— you will not be wholly dependent on my bequest. I want you all to understand that U.S. Government Bonds are the best investment even if the return is small, and then come Commonwealths and Municipals, that have never failed to meet their interest charges. As the years gather you will meet some pretty good salesmen who will try to sell you everything from stock in a copper or gold mine to some patent that they will tell you will bring you millions, but remember, that for every dollar made that way, millions have been lost. I have been taken by this same gentry but that was perhaps because I had to learn from experience—when my father died, my hopes were high, but the exchequer low, and the stock market was on the other side of the railroad tracks, as far as I was concerned.

To Kell, I want to say that if there is anything to this Mendelian theory, you will probably like to bet on a horse or indulge in other forms of gambling—so if you do, never bet what you cannot afford to lose and if you are a loser, don't plunge to try to recoup. That is wherein the danger lies. "There will be another deal, my son, and after that, another one." Just be moderate in all things and don't deal in excesses. (The girls can also take that advice.) I am not going to try to regulate your lives, as nothing is quite as boring as too many "don'ts." I am merely setting down the benefit of my experience, which most people will admit was rather broad, since it runs from Port Said to Hawaii, Miami Beach to South America.

I have written this Will in a lighter vein because I have always felt that Wills were so dreary that they might have been written by the author of "Inner Sanctum" and I can see no reason for it, particularly in my case. My family is raised and I am leaving enough so they can face life with a better than average start, financially.

As for me, just shed a respectful tear if you think I merit it, but I am sure that you are all intelligent enough not to weep all over the place: I have watched a few emotional acts at graves, such as trying to jump into it, fainting, etc. but the thoroughbred grieves in the heart. . . .

Not that my passing should occasion any "scenes" for the simple reason that life owes me nothing. I have ranged far and wide, have really run the gamut of life. I have known great sorrow and great joy. I had more than my share of success. Up to this writing my wife and children have not given me any heartaches, but on the contrary, have given me much happiness and a pardonable pride, and I want them to know I appreciate that. I worked hard in my early life, but I was well paid for that effort.

In this document I can only give you things, but if I had the choice to give you worldly goods or character, I would give you character. The reason I say that, is with character you will get worldly goods because character is loyalty, honesty, ability, sportsmanship and, I hope, a sense of humor.

If I don't stop soon, this will be as long as *Gone With the Wind*, so just remember, when I shove off for greener pastures or whatever it is on the other side of the curtain, that I do it unafraid and, if you must know, a little curious.

Jack Kelly dictated his will to a stenographer on April 14, 1960. He read through the typed manuscript and when he was satisfied that everything was in order he signed it with a flourish—in green ink.

✳

The rest is silence.

HAMLET'S FINAL WORDS